8   Inclusion is about engendering a sense of community and belonging and encouraging mainstream and special schools and others to come together to support each other and pupils with special educational needs. Inclusive schools and local education authorities have:

a. an inclusive ethos;
b. a broad and balanced curriculum for all pupils;
c. systems for early identification of barriers to learning and participation; and
d. high expectations and suitable targets for all children.

a. An inclusive ethos

Schools and local education authorities can use tools like the CSIEs **Index for Inclusion**[7] to identify and remove the barriers to learning and participation. Schools that have adopted this sort of approach have seen standards rise for all of their pupils.

Case Study 1 – Girlington Primary School

Girlington is an inner-city primary school in Bradford. It caters for 500 pupils aged 3-11 years. In total 97% of pupils are bilingual, up to 16 pupils are profoundly deaf and the school educates many pupils with diverse special educational needs. In September 2001 60 of its pupils had been identified as having special educational needs of which 22 had statements.

In September 1998 the school set out on a journey of school improvement based on self-review. Staff used the Index for Inclusion to identify, share and build on their existing knowledge of the barriers that inhibit pupils from learning and participating. The Index helped staff to focus on issues for development that might otherwise have been overlooked including the need to utilizing under-used and often under-valued resources within the staff, parents and the wider school community. The index was used as a tool to challenge and improve development planning to raise standards.

As a result, key stage 1 assessments for English and Maths have increased by 35% over the last three years. Their results are now above national averages at key stage 1. Girlington's pupils, parents, staff and governors continue the daily task of making often small adjustments to welcome all pupils into a climate of achievement and inclusion.

OFSTED inspections monitor how inclusive schools and local education authorities are. OFSTED defines an educationally inclusive school as 'one in which the teaching and learning, achievements, attitudes and well-being of every young person matter.' In order for a school to be satisfactory or better it must be, "inclusive in its policies, outlook and practices"[8]. OFSTED inspections also assess how well a school reaches out to all its learners and the practical steps schools are taking in and out of the classroom in order to take account of pupils' varied life experiences and needs.

Local education authorities are expected to plan strategically and adopt an integrated approach to ensure greater inclusion. They are expected to support, empower and challenge their schools to become more inclusive. Local education authorities need to be open and clear about their plans to develop inclusion and the role of special schools. School Organisation

---

[7] A copy of the Index for Inclusion was sent to all schools in April 2000.
[8] Extract from the OFSTED Secondary and Primary Schools Handbook for Inspecting (page 14).

Plans, Asset Management Plans, Education Development Plans (EDPs), Behaviour Support Plans and Early Years and Child Development Plans (cross-referenced as necessary) should be utilised to plan for inclusion.

Inclusion clearly has training implications. Local education authorities and others can help schools develop and train their staff[9]. Inclusion is a key theme of the **Standards Fund**. The fund should be utilised to support training and development to facilitate inclusion. Training events can highlight successful practice, exploring experience of inclusion and what works. Events might also focus on awareness-raising in relation to particular special educational needs, responding to pupils changing needs or exploring aspects of good practice in terms of joint working.

Arranging joint training sessions with other professionals such as health service staff may be a helpful way of furthering professional understanding and of improving provision made for individual children through better joint working. Local voluntary groups and parents can be invited to take part in training sessions. **The National SEN Specialist Standards** published by the Teacher Training Agency in December 1999 include an accessible audit tool to identify specific teacher training and development needs. The Standards are specifically designed to support the developing role of teachers in an inclusive environment. A related CD-ROM is under development by the Teacher Training Agency.

b. A broad and balanced curriculum for all pupils

All maintained schools and local education authorities must have regard to the **National Curriculum 2000** which incorporates a statement on **Inclusion: providing effective opportunities for all children**. This states that in planning and teaching the National Curriculum teachers have responsibility for:

- setting suitable learning challenges;
- responding to pupils' diverse learning needs; and
- overcoming potential barriers to learning and assessment for individuals and groups of pupils.

The general and subject guidelines on planning, teaching and assessing the curriculum for pupils with learning difficulties, produced by **The Qualifications and Curriculum Authority** (QCA) help schools and others differentiate the curriculum.

c. Systems for early identification of barriers to learning and participation

The **SEN Code of Practice** provides a clear framework for identifying, assessing and meeting pupils' special educational needs. In addition the SEN Code of Practice is supported by a separate toolkit. The toolkit provides schools and local education authorities with detailed advice on day-to-day issues and provides examples of good practice on particular issues. The forthcoming National Performance Framework for SEN aims to provide key SEN data about every local education authority; and set a series of questions for local education authorities to consider as they compare their performance with similar local education authorities.

---

[9] Training is also provided by the voluntary sector – annex B provides some useful websites.

d. High expectations and suitable targets for all children

All schools, helped by their local education authority, are required to set measurable targets. Governing bodies of schools for pupils with large numbers of pupils with special educational needs who in the past might have set zero-rated targets must now set measurable targets[10]. **Supporting The Target Setting Process (Revised March 2001)**, published by the DfEE and QCA, provides guidance on effective target setting for pupils with special educational needs; the guidance is also known as the "P Scales".

Schools (perhaps in clusters) and local education authorities also need to develop systems for aggregating these targets to monitor their success in enabling all pupils to make progress and come close to or reach their personal potential.

The Government is committed to supplementing the information already published in performance tables with information about how far schools, including special schools, help their pupils to progress between the various stages of their education. The **performance tables** will, after piloting work, include value added measures from 2002 for secondary schools and from 2003 for primary schools.

9   The documents listed above and others that can help schools develop to become more inclusive are listed at **annex B**.

Disability equality

10   As well as strengthening the right to a mainstream education the Special Educational Needs and Disability Act 2001 amends the Disability Discrimination Act 1995 and delivers comprehensive enforceable civil rights for disabled pupils and students. The Act ensures that access to school education (as well as further and higher education) is covered by the Disability Discrimination Act 1995. It also covers the admission of disabled pupils to schools, and the education and associated services to pupils. Schools and local education authorities have new duties to prevent discrimination, which will help facilitate inclusion.

11   From September 2002 schools and local education authorities must:

a. not treat disabled pupils less favourably, without justification, for a reason which relates to their disability;

b. make reasonable steps to ensure that disabled pupils are not placed at a substantial disadvantage compared to other pupils who are not disabled (but there is no duty to remove or alter physical features or provide auxiliary aids or services); and

c. also plan strategically for and make progress in improving the physical environment of schools for disabled children, increasing disabled pupils' participation in the curriculum and improving the ways in which written information which is provided to pupils who are not disabled is also provided to disabled pupils.

The Disability Discrimination Act 1995, as amended, gives the Disability Rights Commission the power to issue a Code of Practice in relation to duties imposed on schools. A finalised Code should be available for schools to assist them when the new duties come into force in

---

[10] Targets must be set by December 2001 to take effect from 2003. Target Setting For Pupils with Special Educational Needs (DfEE 0088/2001) provides greater guidance (see annex B for further details).

September 2002. The Department for Education and Skills is also preparing guidance on the duty to plan to make schools more accessible (C. above). Both documents are scheduled to issue during the spring term 2002.

The voice of pupils

12   The **United Nations Convention On The Rights Of The Child** underlines that children who are capable of forming views have a right to receive and make known information, to express an opinion, and have that opinion taken into account in any matters affecting them. The **SEN Code of Practice**[11] highlights the importance of children and young people participating in all the decisions about their education. It makes clear that schools, local education authorities and others should seek to ascertain the views of children and young people about their needs and aspirations and how they might like their needs to be met, as part of statutory assessments. The views of the child should be given due weight when considering whether or not he /she should be educated in a mainstream school.

Working in partnership with parents

13   Parents hold key information and have a critical role to play in their children's education. Chapter 2 of the SEN Code of Practice underlines that it is essential that all professionals actively seek to work with parents and value the contribution they make. This is particularly important when deciding where children with special educational needs should be educated. Chapter 2 also covers the role of **parent partnership services**. These services are designed to ensure that parents whose children have special educational needs have access to accurate, neutral information on their rights, roles and responsibilities. They must provide full information to parents of the wide range of options that are available for their children's education.

14   Inclusion can be an emotive issue. Decisions about the choice of school for a child with special educational needs have real sensitivities for parents. Where parents feel that their views have not been respected or listened to there can be disagreement. All local education authorities must make informal arrangements to **avoid and resolve disagreements**. These can help solve problems and differences of opinion. Parents also have the right of appeal to the SEN Tribunal in certain circumstances, including where they disagree over the educational provision set out in a child's statement.

Safeguarding the needs of pupils with Special Educational Needs

15   Summarised below are the existing safeguards which protect the interests of children with special educational needs. **These must be kept in mind at all times**. The SEN Framework[12] is designed to make sure that pupils' needs are identified and action is taken to ensure they make progress towards reaching their personal potential.

---

[11] Chapter 3 – Pupil Participation provides advice on ascertaining and considering the views of pupils.
[12] As set out in the Education Act 1996, relevant regulations, the SEN Code of Practice and other guidance.

16 The safeguards which protect the interests of pupils with special educational needs are:

- **Parents** must ensure their children receive full-time education suitable to their age, ability, aptitude and any special educational needs they may have. This means that parents need to consider what type of provision is most appropriate for meeting their child's needs. Parent partnership services provide information to parents on the options and empower them to make informed decisions. *(Section 7 of the Education Act 1996)*

- **Local education authorities** must have regard to the general principle that pupils must be educated in accordance with the wishes of their parents, so far as that is compatible with the provision of efficient instruction and training and the avoidance of unreasonable public expenditure. *(Section 9 of the Education Act 1996)*

- **Local education authorities** must ensure that sufficient schools are available for their area and in doing so must have regard to the need to secure special educational provision. Each year authorities must submit for approval, to their local School Organisation Committee, a School Organisation Plan setting out how they will secure sufficient provision. This includes the provision proposed for children with special educational needs and should take account of parental preferences for particular styles of provision or education settings. *(Section 14 of the Education Act 1996 and Section 26) of the School Standards and Framework Act 1998)*

- **Governing Bodies** of maintained schools, and local education authorities in the case of maintained nursery schools, must use their best endeavours to secure that any pupil who has special educational needs receives the special educational provision their learning difficulty calls for. This includes ensuring that teachers are aware of the importance of identifying, and providing for, pupils with special educational needs. *(Section 317 of the Education Act 1996)*

- Where necessary statements of special educational needs should be maintained by **local educational authorities**. Statements specify the provision to be made for a child's special educational needs and local education authorities then have a statutory duty to arrange for it to be made. *(Section 324 of the Education Act 1996)*

- The **Secretary of State for Education and Skills** can intervene where local education authorities or maintained schools are acting unreasonably or failing to fulfil a statutory duty, or where local education authorities are failing to perform their functions to an adequate standard. (The Secretary of State's powers of intervention are discussed further at paragraph 54 below). *Sections 496, 497 and 497A of the Education Act 1996*

- The individual **needs of the child** (who has special educational needs) must be taken into account in deciding whether to name a parent's choice of maintained school (mainstream or special) in a statement. *Schedule 27 of the Education Act 1996*

Inter-agency/Sector partnerships

17 The **SEN Code of Practice**[13] highlights the importance of inter-agency/sector working to support pupils with special educational needs. Education, health and social services together with the voluntary and private sectors need to work together to combine their efforts on behalf

---

[13] See Chapter 10 – Working In Partnership With Other Agencies of the SEN Code of Practice.

of pupils and students. The network of SEN Regional Partnerships – being sponsored by the Department for Education and Skills – are championing new ways of working with the aim of reducing the variations in the quality of response which pupils with similar needs receive. One of the Partnerships' four strategic areas of work is to develop through collaborative working more inclusive policies and practices. The Health Act 1999 flexibilities aim to improve services for users through pooled funds and the delegation of functions (lead commissioning and integrated provision). They are permissive powers to support better co-ordination and innovative approaches to securing services across a wide range of local authority and NHS functions in response to local situations and needs.

How the statutory framework for inclusion works

To which children do sections 316, 316A and Schedule 27 apply?

18 The statutory framework for inclusion applies to any child who should be educated in a school. It does not apply to children being educated at home by their parents or other pupils whose circumstances would normally prevent them from being in school. For example a child receiving in-patient psychiatric treatment or in secure accommodation.

What is a mainstream school?

19 A mainstream school is any school that is not a special school or an independent school. Exceptionally, City Technology Colleges, City Colleges for the Technology of the Arts and City Academies all count as mainstream schools as do Pupil Referral Units[14].

Deciding where children who don't have statements are educated

20 Children who have special educational needs but do not have a statement must, except in the specific circumstances outlined below, be educated in a mainstream school. This has always been the case. The Code of Practice on School Admissions underlines that such pupils must be treated as fairly as other applicants.

   a. Admission authorities must not refuse to admit a child who has special educational needs but does not have a statement because they feel unable to cater for their special educational needs.

   b. Admission authorities must consider applications from parents of children who have special educational needs but no statement on the basis of the school's published admission criteria. Such children should be considered as part of the normal admissions procedures.

   c. Admission authorities cannot refuse to admit a child on the grounds that he/she does not have a statement of special educational needs or the pupil is currently being assessed for one.

21 There may be a very small minority of cases where a child has special educational needs, but does not have a statement, and where it may be more appropriate for the pupil to attend a special school. The decision to place a child who does not have a statement in a special school should not be taken lightly. Wherever possible pupils' needs should be appropriately provided

---

[14] Section 316(4) defines what is meant by a mainstream school.

for in a mainstream school. The exceptional circumstances[15] where it may be right for a child without a statement to attend a special school are:

a. where the child is being assessed to determine whether a statement of special educational needs should be made and he/she is admitted to a special school for the purposes of the assessment. This must be with the agreement of the child's parent, the local education authority, the head teacher of the special school, and any person who is providing advice as part of the assessment. The child may remain in that special school until[16] a statement is made (at which point he/she must then be educated in accordance with the statement) or until the expiry of ten school days after the local education authority formally informs the child's parents that they do not propose to make a statement;

b. where the child's circumstances have changed. This must be with the agreement of the child's parent, the local education authority, and the head teacher of the special school; and

c. where the child is in hospital and has therefore been admitted to a hospital special school[17]. Hospital schools are only an option where the child is ill and requires hospital treatment.

It must be emphasised that this kind of provision will only be appropriate in a small minority of cases (perhaps as little as one or two cases per authority). Wherever possible children should remain at their mainstream school while they are being assessed.

Deciding where children who have statements are educated

The General Duty

22   The starting point is always that children who have statements will receive mainstream education. The new section 316 stipulates that a child who has special educational needs and a statement **must** be educated in a mainstream school unless this would be incompatible with:

a. **the wishes of the child's parents;**

b. **or the provision of efficient education of other children.**

These are the only reasons why mainstream education can be refused outright.

23   Local education authorities and maintained schools[18] can only deny mainstream education, against parental wishes, on the grounds that it would be incompatible with the efficient education of other children. **A local education authority will only be able to rely on this ground if there are no reasonable steps it, or a school, could take to prevent the incompatibility in a particular school or across its mainstream schools. A school will only be able to rely on this ground if there are no reasonable steps that either it or the local education authority could take to prevent the incompatibility at the school.** Clear evidence must be provided to justify why no reasonable steps can be taken. It is envisaged that it will only be possible to demonstrate this in a small minority of cases.

24   **Mainstream education cannot be refused on the grounds that the child's needs cannot be provided for within the mainstream sector** The general duty assumes that with the right strategies and support most children with special educational needs can be included

---

[15] These are set out at section 316A(2) of the Education Act 1996 – see annex A.

[16] These are set out in The Education (Special Educational Needs)(England) (Consolidation) Regulations 2001

[17] All hospital schools are deemed to be special schools.

[18] The authority for particular schools are set out in section 316A(11) of annex A.

successfully at a mainstream school. The local education authority should be able to provide a mainstream option for all but a small minority of pupils. Local education authorities should look across all of their schools and seek to provide appropriate mainstream provision wherever possible. Readers should also read paragraphs 1.33 to 1.38 of the SEN Code of Practice in relation to its advice on infant class sizes.

25 Its essential that pupils, parents, schools, local education authorities and others including health and social services work together. It is important that the views of the child are sought and taken into account.

26 The flowcharts attached at **annex C** summarise the following arrangements and are designed to be an aide memoire.

When Parents Want Mainstream Provision

27 *Option 1 – Parents Express A Preference For A Maintained Mainstream School:* Local education authorities must explain to parents the arrangements[19] that allow them to express a preference for a particular maintained school (mainstream or special). The local education authority must (in accordance with paragraph 3(3) of **Schedule 27** of the Education Act 1996) name the parents' preferred choice of school in the child's statement unless:

a. the school is unsuitable to the child's age, ability, aptitude, or special educational needs; or

b. the child's attendance at the school would be incompatible with the efficient education of other pupils or the efficient use of resources.

28 Before naming a maintained school in a child's statement the local education authority must consult the school, including sending them a copy of the draft statement. If the school is outside the local education authority's area then the local education authority must also consult the local education authority responsible for the school as well. Schedule 27 (paragraph 3(3)) of the Education Act 1996 has not been changed. Schedule 27 determines whether a parent's preferred choice of maintained school is named in the child's statement. **When a maintained school is named in a child's statement the school must admit the child**[20].

29 It is reasonable to expect a local education authority to be able to provide a mainstream educaton for nearly all children with special educational needs. However, it is not reasonable or practical to expect all schools to provide for every possible type of special educational need. When making decisions about individual schools the Government believes that it is right to consider: what parents want; an individual school's suitability to provide for the needs of the pupil; the impact their inclusion would have on resources and the efficient education of others.

30 Where the parents' do not express a choice or their preferred choice of school is not named in the child's statement **section 316** requires that the local education authority must name another mainstream school. It should look across all of its schools. It can only refuse mainstream education where the child's inclusion would be incompatible with the efficient education of other pupils. In addition the local education authority must demonstrate that there are no reasonable steps it or a maintained school could take to prevent the incompatibility. Parents can appeal against the local education authority's decision.

---

[19] Set out in schedule 1 of regulations 14 & 15 of The Education (Special Educational Needs) (England) (Consolidation) Regulations 2001 as provided for by schedule 27 of the Education Act 1996.

[20] This is required by section 324(5)(b) of the Education Act 1996.

31   *Option 2 – Parents Make Representations For An Independent Mainstream School:* City Technology Colleges[21], City Colleges for the Technology of the Arts and City Academies are all publicly funded independent schools. For the purposes of the statutory framework they are mainstream schools. In particular, City Academies are inclusive schools catering for pupils of all abilities. **All other independent schools for these purposes are not classed as a mainstream school even if they do not predominately cater for pupils with special educational needs**. Parents are able to make representations to have any independent or non-maintained school named in their child's statement. This is discussed in further detail in the following sections.

Where parents have asked for a City Technology College, City College for the Technology of the Arts or a City Academy to be named in their child's statement the local education authority must consider the request. In doing so they must have regard to section 9 of the Education Act 1996. This sets the general principle that pupils must be educated in accordance with what their parents want so far as this is compatible with:

a. the provision of efficient instruction and training;

b. the avoidance of unreasonable public expenditure.

Where the local education authority intends to name an independent mainstream school in a child's statement they should consult and seek consent from the school. **When a City Academy is named in a child's statement they must admit the child**[22]. City Technology Colleges, City Colleges for the Technology of the Arts should also admit the child providing that their admission requirements have been satisfied. Where the local education authority does not agree to name the independent mainstream school in the child's statement, section 316 requires them to name another mainstream school. Again mainstream education can only be refused where the child's inclusion would be incompatible with the efficient education of others and there are no reasonable steps to prevent the incompatibility. Parents can appeal against the local education authority's decision.

32   *Option 3 – Parents Do Not Express A Preference For An Individual Mainstream School:* Where parents want mainstream education, but do not indicate what their preferred choice of school is, the local education authority must decide which mainstream school should be named in the child's statement. Again mainstream education can only be refused where the child's inclusion would be incompatible with the efficient of other pupils and there are no reasonable steps to prevent the incompatibility. Parents can appeal against the local education authority's decision.

33   Similar procedures normally apply when parents ask for the school named in their child's statement to be changed.

When Parents Want Non-Mainstream Education (i.e. A Special School Place)

34   **Where a child has a statement, and the parents do not wish the child to be educated in a mainstream school then the local education authority may educate the child in a special school.** A local education authority normally has a duty to educate a child in a mainstream school; however it is not bound by this duty where a child has a statement *and* mainstream education is against the wishes of his parent. However, this decision is up to the local education authority. They may still name a mainstream school in the child's statement.

---

[21] CTCs and CCTAs operate admission criteria which all pupils including those with SEN must satisfy.
[22] This is required via the Academy's funding agreement with the Secretary of State.

But the parents can also appeal against such a decision to the Special Educational Needs Tribunal[23]. It is important that the views of the child and parents are sought and taken into account. There should be strong and clear reasons for going against what parents want; for example what the parents want is incompatible with efficient education or there is strong evidence from those providing advice during the child's statutory assessment. Again it is important that the views of the child are also sought and taken into account.

35 *Option 1 – Parents Express A Preference For A Maintained Special School:* Where parents express a preference for an individual maintained special school the local education authority must name the parents preferred choice of school in the child's statement unless:

a. the school is unsuitable to the child's age, ability or aptitude or to his special educational needs; or

b. the child's inclusion at the school would be incompatible with the efficient education of other pupils or the efficient use of resources.

Before naming a maintained special school in a statement the local education authority must consult the school, including sending them a copy of the draft statement. **When a maintained special school is named in a child's statement the school must admit the child**[24].

36 Where the parent's preferred choice of maintained special school is not named in the child's statement the local education authority must consider the request for special school education. In doing this the local education authority must have regard to the general duty imposed by section 9 (set out in paragraph 31 above). In addition they must also have regard to the need to arrange suitable special educational provision imposed by section 324 of the Education Act 1996. The authority decides which school (special or mainstream) is named in the child's statement. Parents can appeal against the local education authority's decision.

37 *Option 2 – Parents Make Representations For An Independent or Non-Maintained School:* Parents are able to make representations to have an independent school (approved to cater for pupils with special educational needs) or a non-maintained special school named in their child's statement. Where parents have asked for an independent or non-maintained school to be named in their child's statement the local education authority must consider the request. In doing so they must have regard to section 9 of the Education Act 1996 (set out in paragraph 31 above) and the duty to arrange suitable special educational provision (section 324 of the Education Act 1996). Where the local education authority does not agree to name the independent or non-maintained special school in the child's statement they must name another school (mainstream or special) and in doing so have regard to sections 9 and 324 of the Education Act 1996. Parents can appeal against the local education authority's decision.

38 *Option 3 – Parents Do Not Express A Preference For An Individual Special School:* Where parents have already indicated to the local education authority that they do not want mainstream provision but have not indicated what their preferred choice of school is, the local education authority must decide which school is named in the child's statement. The local education must consider the parents' preference for a special school education having regard to sections 9 and 324 of the Education Act. Parents can appeal against the local education authority's decision.

---

[23] 'A Guide To Appeals' produced by the SEN Tribunal offer advice on the appeals process.
[24] This is required by section 324(5)(b) of the Education Act 1996.

39   Similar procedures normally apply when parents ask for the school named in their child's statement to be changed.

Efficient education

40   **Where a child has a statement mainstream education can only be refused, against parental wishes, where the child's inclusion would be incompatible with the efficient education of other children.** Efficient education means providing for each child a suitable and appropriate education in terms of a child's age, ability, aptitude and any special educational needs he/she may or may not have. Paragraphs 48 – 52 consider instances when it may not be possible to include specific children. Whilst it stresses that cases must be considered on their individual merits it explains that this may include pupils whose behaviour systematically, persistently and significantly threatens the safety of and impedes the learning of others. However, all reasonable steps must be taken to enable pupils to be included without compromising the efficient education of other pupils.

41   When a local education authority is considering whether mainstream education is appropriate (i.e. it is not considering the appropriateness of an individual school) the term 'other children' means children with whom the child with the statement would be likely to come into contact with on a regular day to day basis.

42   When considering individual schools **'other children' is intended to mean the children with whom the child who has a statement will directly come into contact with on a regular day-to-day basis.** For example in a primary school it would often be the child's class or literacy/numeracy group. It would not necessarily mean children in other classes or year groups. In a secondary school it may include the pupil's form or tutor group, pupils in the pupil's subject classes or groups or exceptionally even the entire year group. **'Other children' does not mean children in other schools or pupils who will only occasionally come into contact with the child.**

43   The efficient education caveat – within section 316 – must not be abused. OFSTED will be monitoring how schools and local education authorities operate the new inclusion framework. The Secretary of State will also not hesitate to act if she or he believes a maintained school or local education authority was acting unreasonably and using the caveat inappropriately.

44   Trivial and inappropriate reasons should not be used to deny children who should and could benefit from a mainstream educaton from gaining one. The three cases set out below are just some of the examples where minor reasons have been used to block a child's inclusion. The examples also explain how the barriers to learning and participation were overcome.

A young child with brittle bones who walks using a rollator had been successfully included in a mainstream nursery. She and her parents wanted her to transfer to a mainstream primary school. The school's Victorian accommodation had narrow walkways. For her own safety, her parents asked if she could leave class five minutes before the end of lessons in order to miss the rush in the corridors. It was claimed that this would disrupt lessons and therefore her inclusion at the school would be incompatible with the efficient education of other children. Refusing the child mainstream education on these grounds would be an abuse of the efficient education caveat. It is reasonable to allow the children in these circumstances to leave lessons five minutes early. Reasonable steps can be taken to prevent the disruption this might cause. In this case the school carefully timetabled classes, breaks and meals to ensure the young girl was able to avoided crowded corridors. They also created safe environments for her to mix with her peers during lunch and other breaks. The child's inclusion has been successful.

A child with Downs Syndrome had been attending a mainstream secondary school successfully. However, following an annual review it was agreed that a teaching assistant should support the girl in some of her lessons. One of the girl's subject teachers claimed that having another adult in the classroom would be disruptive and make the child's inclusion incompatible with the efficient education of other children. Refusing the child mainstream education on these grounds would be an abuse of the efficient education caveat. Where a child's statement specifies they should receive support from a teaching assistant the assistant must be allowed into the classroom. Reasonable steps can be taken to ensure the teacher and assistant work effectively together and support each other. The child was included successfully.

A child with a hearing impairment who had been successfully included in a mainstream primary school moved into a new local education authority area. The boy and his parents wanted the child to continue education in a mainstream school. They expressed a preference for the school nearest to their home. In order to allow the child to access lessons his classroom teacher needed to wear a microphone. The school claimed that this would be disruptive and would compromise the efficient education of other children. Refusing the child mainstream education on these grounds would be an abuse of the efficient education caveat. In this case the local education authority argued that wearing the microphone would not disrupt other pupils. Rather it required the teacher to take a modest reasonable step to allow the child to access mainstream education. The authority provided training to staff at the school. They also arranged for someone from a local organisation for the deaf to come and talk to the class and explain why their teacher would now be using a microphone. This allowed pupils to discuss the issues in a supportive environment. The child was welcomed into the school and has been included successfully.

Reasonable steps

45   Mainstream education can only be refused on the grounds that a child's inclusion would be incompatible with the efficient education of others where there are no reasonable steps maintained schools or local education authorities could take to prevent the incompatibility. Education law does not set out what should be taken into account when deciding if a step is reasonable. Of course, what constitutes a reasonable step or steps depends on all of the circumstances of the individual case. Also what can be reasonably expected of schools and local education authorities now will be very different in years to come as they become more able to meet the needs of diverse groups of children. However, without intending to be exhaustive, the following are some of the factors which might be taken into account when considering what is reasonable:

a.   whether taking the step would be effective in overcoming the incompatibility;

b.   the extent to which it is practical for the maintained school or local authority to take the step;

c.   the extent to which steps have already been taken to facilitate the child's inclusion and their effectiveness;

d.   the financial and other resource implications of taking the step; and

e.   the extent of any disruption taking the step would cause.

46   When it comes to considering what is reasonable – i.e. what are the reasonable steps which could be taken by either a maintained school or local education authority or both – the cost implications will be a factor. It will often be reasonable to spend some money. However, it will not always be reasonable to spend large amounts of money. Set out below are some examples of the sorts of reasonable steps school and local education authorities could take to prevent a child's inclusion being incompatible with the efficient education of other children. Pupils with disabilities within the meaning of the Disability Discrimination 1995 will have further protection from September 2002 when the amendments to the Act come into force. Until then pupils with SEN and a disability will only be covered by this inclusion guidance. It is expected that the reasonable steps under the Disability Discrimination Act will be similar to those set out below. This is in no way an exhaustive or definitive list. Rather the examples are designed to help schools and local education authorities think about the sorts of reasonable steps they could take.

The reasonable steps to ensure that the inclusion of a child with learning difficulties is not incompatible with the efficient education of other children may include:

- praising the pupil's strengths and areas of success so that self esteem is maintained and enhanced;

- using flexible grouping arrangements including ones where the pupil can work with more able peers;

- providing for all pupils experiences which will be of benefit to most pupils but particularly to the pupil with learning difficulties;

- considering carefully the use of language in the classroom and strategies to promote the learning of need vocabulary;

- setting appropriate targets so that personal progress can be tracked as well as progress towards externally determined goals;

- considering carefully the pupil's learning styles and ensuring that this is reflected in the styles of teaching; and,

- developing a partnership with the parents to support the pupil and the curriculum.

The reasonable steps to ensure that the inclusion of a primary aged pupil who has severe temper tantrums is not incompatible with efficient education of other children **may** include:

- addressing factors within the *class* that may be contributing to the problem – e.g. addressing teasing by using circle time as a forum for discussing teasing and how to respond to it;

- teaching the child alternative behaviours – i.e. taking quiet time in a specially designated area at times of stress;

- providing the child with a channel of communication other than tantrums – i.e. fetching another child identified as their 'listening partner', or completing a 'think bubble sheet' to identify the stressor, the accompanying feelings and his or her possible courses of action;

- using a carefully designed system of behaviour targets, drawn up together with the child, and linked to a powerful reward system which, wherever possible, involves parents/carers;

- ensuring that all staff who deal with the child have been briefed on potential triggers for outbursts, and effective ways of heading off trouble at an early stage – i.e. an agreed school-wide system where the child is asked to take a colour-coded object to another member of staff as soon as the emotional temperature is rising;

- drawing up a contingency plan for what will happen if there is a confrontation in class: in conjunction with the child, identifying a key helper who will be summoned to remove the child or the rest of the class from the situation, identifying how they will know the need is urgent, and setting out what the later consequences will be for the child if this system has to be used; and

- ensuring that if there is any possibility that positive handling may need to be used to prevent injury to others or damage to property, that relevant staff have had training in appropriate techniques, that these have been carefully explained to the child, and that the circumstances under which they may be used have been recorded on a written plan agreed with and signed by the child and his or her parents/carers.

The reasonable steps to ensure that the inclusion of a secondary aged pupil with Downs Syndrome working towards level 1 of the National Curriculum is not incompatible with efficient education of other children **may** include:

- identifying a named member of staff to oversee the social and curriculum aspects of the pupil's inclusion, and liaise with parents and outside agencies;

- planning an individualised and differentiated curriculum, by identifying links between the content of whole class work and the learning objectives appropriate at pre-Level 1;

- adjusting the balance of the curriculum to allow for additional time to be spent on such areas as expressive and receptive language, personal, social and life skills;

- arranging for in-class support from a teaching assistant and securing appropriate training for the teaching assistant, from the local education authority or other sources;

- training subject teachers in using teaching styles which include visual prompts to support curriculum delivery, delivering instructions in short chunks and checking for understanding, giving the pupil time to process language and respond;

- providing for alternative means of access to tasks involving reading and writing;

- ensuring access to appropriate ICT – for example, talking word processor software;

- encouraging peer support – for example, by setting up a 'circle of friends' who have chosen to plan ways in which they can help the pupil access the curriculum and the social opportunities provided by the school;

- adhere to teaching timetables, routines and school rules explicitly, and allowing the pupil time to learn them; and

- arranging for a key worker to meet regularly with the pupil to discuss positives and difficulties, build on successes and sustain meaningful links with home.

The reasonable steps to ensure that the inclusion of a secondary aged pupil with emotional and behavioural difficulties whose behaviour is not incompatible with efficient education of other children **may** include:

- identifying a key worker in school whose role is to meet regularly with the pupil to build the relationship, monitor progress, pull together multi-agency support, pass on relevant information to staff, and mediate between pupil and teacher where relationships are strained;

- ensuring close home-school links so that the school are immediately aware of changes to the home situation which may limpact on the child's behaviour and can make special arrangements where this occurs;

- providing for the pupil to attend an in-school support centre either full time during periods of stress, or on the basis of withdrawal from lessons which are particular trouble-spots;

- providing the pupil with a carefully structured and monitored way of withdrawing him or herself from difficult situations for example, use of a sanctuary card for access to an in-school centre or quiet *'cool-off'* area;

- arranging one-to-one or group work where conflict resolution strategies can be discussed and role-played;

- involving the pupil in a planned programme to build self-esteem, such as tutoring younger pupils or being part of a group that counsels or supports pupils who are experiencing friendship problems;

- ensuring that all staff who teach the pupil have shared, and are briefed on, effective strategies to deal with overt challenge, for example phrasing instructions as choices (*'put the magazine on my desk or in your bag'*), avoiding language which might make the pupil feel publicly shamed, constructing face-saving ways out for a pupil who has backed him or herself into a corner;

- ensuring that all staff have had training in de-escalation techniques for dealing with parents or pupils; and

- ensuring that an emergency plan is in place through which all staff can summon assistance if needed.

The reasonable steps to ensure that the inclusion of a pupil whose special educational needs mean that he/she has severe difficulties in sitting still and focusing attention is not incompatible with efficient education of other children **may** include:

- providing a distraction-free work area on the edge of the group;

- ensuring peer support, for example by enlisting a 'circle of friends' who identify and use strategies to help the child sustain concentration;

- adapting the length and nature of tasks, for example, using alternatives to paper and pencil tasks, if extended periods of writing are a particular source of difficulty;

- alternating periods of concentration with the opportunity to move around and change activity;

- providing in-class support for lessons which are particularly problematic; and

- using an individually tailored behaviour management structure where the consequences of disrupting others' work are cumulative and clear, and the rewards for concentration carefully planned.

The reasonable steps to ensure that the inclusion of a child with an autistic spectrum disorder who is noisy and often runs around the classroom is not incompatible with the efficient education of other children **may** include:

- ensuring that all possible steps have been taken to ensure structure and predictability in the child's day – for example, use of visual timetables, careful prior explanation of any changes to routine, use of closed rather than open-ended tasks;

- ensuring that the child is explicitly taught a means of communicating wants and needs using sign, symbol or spoken language;

- using a workstation outside the class in which the child can have a calm and quiet start to a session, working with a teaching or learning support assistant on a structured programme of activities designed to prepare him or her for joining in the class activities – for example, using 'social scripts' to rehearse appropriate classroom behaviours;

- providing the child with an individual workstation in class, where distractions are kept to a minimum and everything needed for the work to be done organised in sequence;

- using a clear visual behaviour management plan in a discrete area of the classroom, for example *'three strikes and you're out'* illustrated on a velcro board, alongside an equally clear and fairly immediate visual reward system; and

- ensuring that all staff are briefed on the warning signs that may indicate potential behavioural challenge, and on a range of activities which provide effective distraction if used sufficiently early.

Instances when it may not be possible to include specific children

47   **Readers are reminded that this section only applies to pupils who have statements.** Children who have special educational needs but do not have statements must be educated in mainstream schools apart from in exceptional circumstances (see paragraph 21 above). The Code of Practice on School Admissions states[25] that admission authorities should not make subjective judgements. If a pupil, once admitted, is found to be seriously and persistently disruptive, then the school may consider disciplinary action, including temporary or permanent exclusion procedures. **It is also unacceptable for a school to refuse to admit a child thought to be potentially disruptive, or to exhibit challenging behaviour, on the grounds that the child ought first to be assessed for special educational needs.**

Strategies To Support Specific Children

48   Behaviour Support Plans and other strategies used by schools and local education authorities should tackle occasional or spasmodic inappropriate behaviour. Schools and local education authorities also need to consider whether their policies and practices act as barriers to some learners which can lead to inappropriate or challenging behaviour. For example where a child finds it difficult to access the curriculum or other aspects of the school's life this could lead to poor behaviour. Removing the barrier and allowing the pupil to access the curriculum may also address the child's poor behaviour. Where a child's primary needs are normally supported in mainstream schools and he/she is presenting challenging behaviour, this may be due to a variety of reasons which could include the child being bullied or he/she is not being fully engaged in or challenged by the school's curriculum. In such cases there should be reasonable steps the school and local education authority could take to prevent the child's inclusion or continuing inclusion being incompatible with the efficient education of other pupils.

49   Learning Support Units or short-term use of Pupil Referral Units can also play a significant part in ensuring that pupils are able to remain in mainstream education, or make a successful return to mainstream following exclusion. Schools and local education authorities need to share good practice in supporting pupils who present challenging and disruptive behaviour. Schools can draw on the expertise of special schools – particularly those who cater for pupils with emotional and behavioural problems – and Pupil Referral Units.

50   Pupil Support (circular 10/99) provides additional practical guidance on pupil attendance, behaviour, exclusion and re-integration. This includes advice on handling signs of disaffection and managing disruptive behaviour that can be used to help ensure children can continue within mainstream schools.

51   All reasonable steps must be taken to enable pupils to be included without compromising the efficient education of other pupils. The decision not to educate a pupil in a mainstream school – against their parent's wishes – should not be taken lightly. It is important that all cases are judged on the individual circumstances. There may be a range of reasons where it may not always be possible to take reasonable steps to prevent a child's inclusion being incompatible with the efficient education of others. For example:

---

[25] Paragraphs 5.21. – 5.24 of the Code of Practice On School Admissions.

a. a child's behaviour systematically, persistently and significantly threatens the safety of others; and,

b. a child's behaviour systematically, persistently and significantly impedes the learning of others.

An extreme incident may be sufficient to make the child's inclusion incompatible with the efficient education of others where it is highly likely that it would occur again and there are no reasonable steps that could be taken to prevent this.

52   There may also be cases where a child's inclusion would mean, even with other support – for example from a teaching assistant – that the teacher had to spend a greatly disproportionate amount of time with the child, in relation to the rest of the class. For example a child who constantly seeks attention from the teacher that persistently and significantly impacts on others learning and cannot be circumvented by alternative strategies. Again, pupils who occasionally require more time should not be refused a mainstream education as it should be possible to take reasonable steps to address the issue and safeguard the efficient education of others.

Special schools

53   The Government recognises and values the important role special schools (maintained, independent and non-maintained) play in providing for pupils with special educational needs. Special schools have a continuing and vital role to play within an inclusive education system. All special schools must be outward looking centres of excellence working with their mainstream partners and other special schools to support the development of inclusion. The strengthened right to a mainstream educaton, provided by the new statutory framework for inclusion, does not make it any harder for parents, whose children have statements, to obtain a place in a special school if that is what they want. It is important that what parents and children want is listened to and taken account of.

Case study 2 – Meath School

Meath is a non-maintained special school in Surrey run by ICAN. The school caters for pupils aged between 5-12 who have speech and language difficulties and associated difficulties. The school has developed close links with a number of local education authorities and mainstream schools.

As part of their outreach programme the school has worked with a mainstream school in a London borough to enable the successful inclusion of a child. The child's parents initially wanted the child to attend Meath. However, the school assessed the pupil's needs and felt his needs could be appropriately provided for within a mainstream school. Meath's Curriculum and Assessment Leader and Head of Speech and Language Therapy provided training to the mainstream school's teachers, SENCO, teacher assistants and the child's parents. The training was well received and the child has been successfully included. The links between the two schools have also benefited Meath. The training package can be adapted and offered again to support the inclusion of other children.

CASE Study 3 – Norfolk Park School

Norfolk Park School in Sheffield caters for children with severe and complex learning difficulties aged between 2 and 11 years. Over the years the school has developed a strategy for good inclusive practice by working closely with parents and children, teachers in mainstream schools and other professionals. They provide support, advice and in-service training across the city. This flexible and adaptable approach has shaped the way in which they have defined their role as a special school. Their inclusion programme was highly praised by OFSTED in their recent school inspection reporting that the school provides excellent support to enable pupils with a wide range of special educational needs to be included in mainstream schools.

The school inclusion team is responsible for providing the opportunity for every pupil within the school to work alongside their mainstream peers in a variety of ways depending on individual needs. Some children are dually registered at Norfolk Park and their local mainstream school, whilst others are successfully supported in their own community school for one or two sessions a week. OFSTED reported that, "This not only contributes significantly to their learning but is also a significant factor in their personal and social development." In addition they have also made various links with local schools where part or whole classes join together to share literacy/numeracy hours, topics, social events and resources on a regular basis.

As part of their outreach role, the team have set up a very successful Inclusion Forum that provides opportunities for support and networking for professionals across the city. They also provide general support for mainstream schools and parents regarding individual pupils as well as inclusive issues in general. To enhance this support the school have produced a practical document to guide and support teachers and other professionals in developing their inclusive practices. Within this document general inclusive issues are addressed alongside practical teaching suggestions, class and whole school strategies and other useful information. The school has developed two training videos entitled 'Meaning for Inclusion' and 'The Changing Role of Special schools' – to share their expertise and experience.

Independent schools and non-maintained special schools

54   The arrangements by which a child with a statement can be placed and funded by a local education authority in an independent school approved to cater for children with special educational needs or a non-maintained special school have also not been changed. Parents whose children have statements, and those for whom a statement is being drawn up, continue to be able to make representations for their child's statement to name an independent or non-maintained school. The local education authority must give full consideration to the parent's representations. Where a local education authority names an independent or non-maintained special school in a child's statement the local education authority must fund the placement.

55   In placing children at independent schools, under section 347 of the Education Act 1996 the school must be approved by the Secretary of State for Education and Skills or the Secretary of State should have given his consent to the child being educated there (see subsection (5)). Section 348 will apply where the local education authority are satisfied that the child's interests require education at a non-maintained school and that education at the particular school is

appropriate. Where a local education authority disagrees with what parents want and does not name the independent or non-maintained school in the child's statement the parents have the right of appeal to the SEN Tribunal.

56   **Nothing in the new inclusion framework affects a local education authority's duties in respect of funding non-maintained placements**. Where appropriate statements should name non-maintained schools and independent schools approved to cater for children with special educational needs. Parents whose children have special educational needs continue to have the right to educate their child, at their own expense, at an independent school or non-maintained special school if they so choose[26].

Education otherwise

57   The new statutory framework for inclusion does not affect parents' right to educate their children outside of the school system[27].

Dual placements

58   The appropriate use of dual placements[28] – where a child can attend more than one school – can support inclusion. It can help prepare pupils for mainstream education and prepare schools to meet the child's needs. Dual placements can also allow children time away from their mainstream school for specialist or catch up support. The new inclusion framework does not inhibit in any way the appropriate use of dual placements. One of the case studies in **Connecting Schools for Inclusion** – an interactive CD ROM training package looking at how mainstream and special schools can work together – looks at the role of dual placements in supporting pupils with special educational needs.

59   In order for a pupil with special educational needs who is being supported by a dual placement to be deemed as being educated at a mainstream school the pupil must spend the majority – i.e. 51% or more – of their time at a mainstream school. Where a pupil is being supported back into a mainstream school via a dual placement the pupil's statement should be amended to name the mainstream school at the point the child is ready to spend 51% or more of their time at the mainstream school.

60   The Education (Pupil Registration) Regulations 1995 were amended from 1 September 2001 to ensure that when a pupil is attending their dual placement school he/she is recorded as participating in an approved educational activity instead of as an 'authorised absent' as previously occurred.

---

[26] This is guaranteed by section 316A(1) of the Education Act 1996.

[27] This right is guaranteed by section 7 and 316 of the Education Act 1996.

[28] Permitted by the Education (Pupils Registration) Regulations 1995, as amended, provided for by section 434 of the Education Act 1996.

Monitoring

Ofsted

61 Her Majesty's Chief Inspector of Schools (HMCI) will be monitoring the impact of the new inclusion framework. In particular HMCI will be looking at how section 316(3)(a) parental wishes and section 316(3)(b) efficient education operate. OFSTED school inspections monitor how inclusive schools are. The joint local educational authority inspections undertaken by OFSTED and the Audit Commission monitor how the authorities are supporting and facilitating inclusion and the quality of provision they make for pupils with special educational needs.

The Secretary of State's powers of intervention

62 The Secretary of State for Education and Skills can intervene[29] where local education authorities or maintained schools are acting unreasonably, failing to fulfil a statutory duty, or where local education authorities are failing to perform their functions to an adequate standard. This includes intervention to safeguard the interests of pupils with special educational needs. Set out below are some examples where the Secretary of State has used these powers.

> Section 497 was used to direct a maintained school to admit a child whose statement named the school. This was the parents preferred choice of school. The school's failure to admit the child meant they were in default of a statutory duty. In reaching this decision the Secretary of State had to consider the school's suitability for the child's age, ability, and special educational needs.

> The Secretary of State asked officials to call a local education authority in for a meeting because it had been alleged they were operating a blanket policy not to quantify provision in statements. Another local education authority was called in because the Department was alerted to a case where a child had been out of school for a long period of time because of a dispute over the school to be named in the pupil's statement. The meetings were held on the basis that the authorities had been called in to justify why the Secretary of State's powers of intervention should not be used.

Further information and reading

63 Annex B lists a series of useful documents and other resources (including websites) which can help schools and local education authorities remove the barriers to learning and participation.

Acknowledgements

64 The Department for Education and Skills would like to thank all of the pupils, parents, teachers, voluntary groups, the network of SEN Regional Partnerships and officers from local education authorities and professional associations who have helped produce this guidance.

Department for Education and Skills
October 2001

---

[29] Sections 496, 497 and 497A of the Education Act 1996 set out the Secretary of State's powers of intervention.

Annex A – Sections 316 and 316A of the Education Act 1996

Section 1 of the Special Education Needs and Disability Act 2001 amends section 316 of the 1996 Act to read:

316 Duty to educate children with special educational needs in mainstream schools

(1) This section applies to a child with special educational needs who should be educated in a school.

(2) If no statement is maintained under section 324 for the child, he must be educated in a mainstream school.

(3) If a statement is maintained under section 324 for the child, he must be educated in a mainstream school unless that is incompatible with –

    (a) the wishes of his parent, or

    (b) the provision of efficient education for other children.

(4) In this section and section 316A "mainstream school" means any school other than –

    (a) a special school, or

    (b) an independent school which is not –

        (i) a city technology college,

        (ii) a city college for the technology of the arts, or

        (iii) a city academy.

Section 1 of the Special Education Needs and Disability Act 2001 also inserts a new section 316A into the 1996 Act:

316A Education otherwise than in mainstream schools

(1) Section 316 does not prevent a child from being educated in –

    (a) an independent school which is not a mainstream school, or

    (b) a school approved under section 342,

    if the cost is met otherwise than by a local education authority.

(2) Section 316(2) does not require a child to be educated in a mainstream school during any period in which –

    (a) he is admitted to a special school for the purposes of an assessment under 323 of his educational needs and his admission to that school is with the agreement of –

        (i) the local education authority,

        (ii) the head teacher of the school or, if the school is in Wales, its governing body,

        (iii) his parent, and

        (iv) any person whose advice is to be sought in accordance with regulations made under paragraph 2 of schedule 26;

    (b) he remains admitted to a special school, in prescribed circumstances, following an assessment under section 323 at the school;

    (c) he is admitted to a special school, following a change in his circumstances, with the agreement of –

        (i) the local education authority,

        (ii) the head teacher of the school or, if the school is in Wales, its governing body, and

        (iii) his parent;

(d) he is admitted to a community or foundation special school which is established in a hospital.

(3) Section 316 does not effect the operation of –

(a) section 348, or

(b) paragraph 3 of schedule 27.

(4) If a local education authority decide –

(a) to make a statement for a child under section 324, but

(b) not to name in the statement the school for which a parent has expressed a preference under paragraph 3 of schedule 27, they shall, in making the statement, comply with section 316(3).

(5) A local education authority may, in relation to their mainstream schools taken as a whole, rely on the exception in section 316(3)(b) only if they show that there are no reasonable steps that they could take to prevent the incompatibility.

(6) An authority in relation to a particular mainstream school may rely on the exception in section 316(3)(b) only if it shows that there are no reasonable steps that it could or another authority in relation to the school could take to prevent the incompatibility.

(7) The exception in section 316(b) does not permit a governing body to fail to comply with the duty imposed by section 324(5)(b).

(8) An authority must have regard to guidance about section 316 and this section issued –

(a) for England, by the Secretary of State,

(b) for Wales, by the National Assembly for Wales.

(9) That guidance shall, in particular, relate to steps which may, or may not, be regarded as reasonable for the purposes of subsections (5) and (6).

(10) "Prescribed", in relation to Wales, means prescribed in regulations made by the National Assembly for Wales.

(11) "Authority" –

(a) in relation to a maintained school, means each of the following –

(i)   the local education authority,

(ii) the school's governing body, and

(b) in relation to a maintained nursery school or a pupil referral unit, means the local education authority.

Annex B – Useful documents and further reading

Most unpriced documents can be obtained from the **DfES Publications Centre**, PO Box 5050, Sherwood Park, Annesley, Nottinghamshire NG15 0DJ. Tel. 0845 6022260 Fax 0845 6033360 Minicom 0845 60555650 E-mail dfes@prolog.uk.com

Priced documents can usually be obtained from **The Stationery Office** at: PO Box 29, Norwich, NR3 1GN Tel 0870 600 5522; Fax 0870 600 5533; website www.thestationeryoffice.com

Publications are listed in alphabetical order of the publisher/lead organisation:

Centre for Studies on Inclusive Education: Index for Inclusion 2000 £24.95. The DfEE funded the distribution of one copy of the Index to all schools, local education authorities and main Initial Teacher Training Institutions in April 2000. The Index helps schools identify the barriers to learning and participation. Further information and copies of the Index can be obtained from CSIE, Room 2S 203, S Block, Frenchay Campus, Coldharbour Lane, Bristol BS16 1QU Tel 0117 344 4007 Fax 0117 344 4005 Website www.inclusion.org.uk

DfEE: Code of Practice on School Admissions published April 1999 sets out what schools and local education authorities have to do when admitting pupils. Unpriced sent to schools and local education authorities and available from DfES publications reference CPSA

DfEE: Code of Practice on School Admission Appeals published September 1999 sets out the arrangements for the appeals process. Unpriced sent to schools and local education authorities and available from DfES publications reference SAACP

DfEE: Connecting Schools for Inclusion an interactive CD Rom which looks at strengthening links between special and mainstream schools to support the inclusion of pupils with SEN. Unpriced, copies sent to all local education authorities, loan copies available for schools. Available from Voluntary Partnerships Team, SEN Division, DfES tel 020 7925 6881 fax 020 7925 5920

DfEE: Inclusive School Design Building Bulletin 94 provides advice and guidance on how to accommodate pupils with special educational needs and disabilities in mainstream schools. Published in 2001 £19.95 available from the Stationery Office. Further information from Architects and Building Branch, DfES, Caxton House, 6-12 Tothill Street, London SW1H 9NA Tel 020 7273 6023; Fax 020 7273 6762; Website www.dfes.gov.uk/schoolbuildings

DfEE: Meeting Special Educational Needs – A Programme of Action 1998 plus termly updates unpriced and sent to all schools, local education authorities, Social Service Departments, Health Authorities and NHS Trusts in England. Available from DfES publication centre and DfES website www.dfes.gov.uk/sen

DfEE: National Curriculum 2000 sets out the curriculum for schools and local education authorities available from www.nc.uk.net

DfEE: Social Inclusion: Pupil Support 10/99 sets out guidance on pupil attendance, behaviour, exclusion and re-integration. Unpriced sent to all schools and local education authorities available from DfES publications centre.

DfEE/DoH: Education of Young People in Public Care which gives guidance on addressing under achievement of children and young people in public care. Unpriced, copies sent to local education authorities and other interested bodies and available from DfES Publications Centre.

DfEE/DoH/NHS: Education of Sick Children Circular 12/94 provides guidance on the education of children unable to attend school because of their medical needs. Unpriced sent to local education authorities and other interested bodies and available from DfES Publications Centre. Revised guidance is scheduled to issue in November 2001.

DfEE/QCA: Supporting the Target Setting Process (Revised March 2001) guidance for effective target setting for pupils with special educational needs 2001. Also known as the 'P scales'. Unpriced available from DfES publications centre or www.standards.dfes.gov.uk

DfES: SEN Code of Practice 2001 Unpriced due to be published December 2001 copies will be sent to all schools and local education authorities. SEN Toolkit copies available from DfES publication centre and www.dfes.gov.uk/sen

Disability Equality in Education: Training for Inclusion & Disability Equality Course Book. Priced This and other resources for inclusion and disability equality are available from DEE, Unit GL, Leroy House, 436 Essex Road, London N1 3 QP. Tel 020 7359 2855; e-mail info@diseed.org.uk; website www.diseed.org.uk

Disability Rights Commission: Code of Practice for Schools final version due to issue to all schools & local education authorities in Spring 2002 priced further details from www.drc-gb.org Tel 08457 622 633

Disability Rights Task Force: Report From Exclusion To Inclusion published in 1999 unpriced available from DfES publication centre and www.disability.gov.uk

HMSO: Education Act 1996 £36.50 available from the Stationery Office

HMSO: School Standards and Framework Act 1998 £19.90 available from the Stationery Office

National Association for Special Educational Needs (NASEN): Inclusion policy document and a variety of other policy documents on special educational needs. Details from NASEN House, 4/5 Amber Business Village, Amber Close, Tamworth B77 4RP Tel: 01827 311500 e-mail welcome@nasen.org.uk; website www.nasen.org.uk

Norfolk Park School: Training Videos 'Meaning for Inclusion' and 'The Changing Role of Special Schools' £5 each available from Glenys Croston or Pauline Zelaieta, Norfolk Park School, Park Grange Road, Sheffield, South Yorkshire S2 3QF Tel 0114 272 6165

OFSTED: Handbooks for Inspecting Schools – separate copies for those inspecting primary schools; secondary schools; special schools and pupil referral units. Published in 2000 £15 each available from the Stationery Office

OFSTED: Evaluating Educational Inclusion – Guidance for inspectors and schools. Unpriced Ref No. HMI 235 available from http://www.ofsted.gov.uk Tel 020 7421 6800

Qualifications and Curriculum Authority: Planning, Teaching and Assessing the Curriculum for Pupils with Learning Difficulties 2001 – general guidance plus individual guides for each National Curriculum subject. Priced and available from QCA Publications PO Box 99, Sudbury, Suffolk CO10 6SN Tel 01787 884 444 or www.nc.uk.net/ld

SEN Tribunal: A Guide To Appeals for parents published September 2001 Unpriced and sent to LEA contacts and other SEN Tribunal users. Available from The Special Educational Needs Tribunal, Secretariat, Windsor House, 7th Floor, 50 Victoria Street, London SW1H 0NW Tel 01325 392 555 or DfES publications centre

The Stationery Office: Special Educational Needs and Disability Act 2001 £7.50 sets out the legal changes to the Education Act 1996 for pupils with SEN and disabilities; Explanatory Notes on the Act explains what the legislation does seting out the position before and after the Act £6.00

Teacher Training Agency: The National SEN Specialist Standards for teachers published in 1999. Unpriced and available from TTA publications tel 0845 606 0323 or www.teach-tta.gov.uk

Useful websites:

BECTA: British Educational Communications and Technology Agency www.becta.org.uk Becta is the Government's lead agency on the use of ICT in education, Becta plays a crucial role in helping to maximise the benefits to all teachers and learners that using ICT can bring. Its main aim is to bridge educational and technological developments and communities. Becta also seeks to:

- Evaluate information and communications technology (ICT) practice

- Support existing applications of ICT

- Investigate emerging technologies and associated pedagogy.

Inclusion website: http://inclusion.ngfl.gov.uk/
This website provides a free catalogue of resources for teaching professionals, learners, parents and carers. Resources include publications, software, hardware, guidance and links to other organisations to aid independent living and learning.

SEN Tribunal: www.sentribunal.gov.uk/
The Special Educational Needs Tribunal was set up by the Education Act 1993. It considers parents' appeals against the decisions of Local Education Authorities (LEAs) about children's special educational needs if parents cannot reach agreement with the LEA. The Tribunal is independent. The Lord Chancellor appoints the President and the chairmen, and the Secretaries of State for Education and Employment and for Wales appoint the members.

SEN Regional Partnerships: www.dfes.gov.uk/sen/index.cfm

The overall aim of the network of eleven SEN regional partnerships – covering England – is to help redress the variations in the responses pupils with similar needs receive. They bring together groups of local educational authorities, health, social services and the voluntary and private sectors to work collaboratively to enhance the way we provide for pupils with special educational needs and ensure services are delivered efficiently.

Contacts for the Regional Partnerships are as follows:

- **Eastern:** www.hertsdirect.org/senregionalproject
- **East Midlands:** www.emleas.org.uk
- **London:** www.londonregionsenproject.org.uk
- **Merseyside:** www.merseysen.org.uk
- **North East:** http://www.inclusion-ne.org.uk/
- **North West:** www.sen-northwest.org.uk
- **South Central:** www.scrip.uk.net
- **South East:** www.sersen.uk.net/main.htm
- **South West:** www.sw-special.co.uk
- **West Midlands:** www.westmidlandsrcp.org.uk
- **Yorkshire and The Humber:** www.yhsen.org.uk

Annex C – Deciding where a child who has a statement is educated

Part 1 – when parents want mainstream provision

1. **Parents consider the type of school/provision they want for their child.**

The Parent Partnership Service is available to provide neutral information on parents' rights, roles and responsibilities and the full range of options available. The views of the child should also be sought and taken into account.

↓

2. **The parents decide they want mainstream education.**

Section 316 of the Education Act 1996 requires the LEA to provide mainstream education unless the child's inclusion would be incompatible with the efficient education of others and there are no reasonable steps can be taken to prevent the incompatibility.

↓ ↓ ↓

3. **Parent express a preference for a particular *maintained* *mainstream* school to be named in their child's statement.**

Schedule 27 of the Education Act 1996 requires the LEA to name the parent's preferred choice of school in the statement unless:

a. the school can not provide for the needs of the child;

b. the child's inclusion at the school would be incompatible with the efficient education of other pupils or the efficient use of resources.

Where the parent's preferred choice is not named section 316 of the Education Act 1996 requires the LEA to name another mainstream school.

3. **Parents make representations for an *independent mainstream* school to be named in their child's statement (a CTC, CCTA or a City Academy)**. For these purposes all other independent schools do not count as a mainstream school.

In considering the parent's request the LEA must have regard to section 9 of the Education Act 1996. This sets the general principle that pupils must be educated in accordance with parental wishes so far as this is compatible with the provision of efficient instruction and training and the avoidance of unreasonable public expenditure.

Where the LEA do not agree to name the independent mainstream school section 316 of the Education Act 1996 requires the LEA to name another mainstream school.

Note: Pupils would still have to satisfy the normal admission criteria that these schools set.

3. **Parents *do not express a preference* for the individual school to be named in their child's statement.**

Section 316 of the Education Act 1996 requires the LEA to decide which mainstream school should be named in the child's statement.

4. Mainstream education can only be refused where the child's inclusion would be incompatible with the efficient education of other pupils and there are no reasonable steps to prevent the incompatibility.

The parents disagree or are unhappy about what the LEA has proposed. (This can occur at any time)

At any stage of the process parents can use the local informal disagreement resolution arrangements, which include an independent element, to seek to resolve any disputes. This service is entered into voluntarily and does not affect the right to lodge a formal appeal to the SEN Tribunal. Where parents disagree with the provision proposed in their child's statement (including the school or type of school) they can appeal to the SEN Tribunal. The local parent partnership service can provide advice and act as a signpost to these services.

The same procedures normally apply when parents ask for the school named in their child's statement to be changed.

Annex C – Deciding where a child who has a statement is educated

Part 2 – when parents want non-mainstream provision

1. **Parents consider the type of school/provision they want for their child**.

The Parent Partnership Service is available to provide neutral information on parents' rights, roles and responsibilities and the full range of options available. The views of the child should also be sought and taken into account.

↓

2. **The parents decide they want non-mainstream education** (i.e. a place in a special school).

The duty imposed on the LEA by section 316 of the Education Act 1996 to educate the child in a mainstream school is lifted.

↓   ↓   ↓

3. **Parent express a preference for a particular *maintained special* school to be named in their child's statement.**	3. **Parents make representations for a *non-maintained school/ independent* to be named in their child's statement**	3. **Parents *do not express a preference* for the individual special school to be named in their child's statement.**

3. Parent express a preference for a particular *maintained special* school to be named in their child's statement.

Schedule 27 requires the LEA to name the parent's preferred choice of school in the statement unless:

a. the school can not provide for the needs of the child;

b. the child's inclusion at the school would be incompatible with the efficient education of other pupils or the efficient use of resources.

If the parent's preferred choice is not named the LEA consider the request for a special school education and name a school in the statement.

The LEA must have regard to section 9 of the Education Act 1996. This sets the general principle that pupils must be educated in accordance with parental wishes so far as this is compatible with the provision of efficient instruction and training and the avoidance of unreasonable public expenditure. The LEA must also have regard to the need to arrange suitable special educational provision imposed by section 324 of the Education Act 1996.

3. Parents make representations for a *non-maintained school/ independent* to be named in their child's statement

In considering the parent's request the LEA must have regard to section 9 of the Education Act 1996. This sets the general principle that pupils must be educated in accordance with parental wishes so far as this is compatible with the provision of efficient instruction and training and the avoidance of unreasonable public expenditure.

The LEA must also have regard to the need to arrange suitable special educational provision imposed by section 324 of the Education Act 1996.

Where the LEA does not agree to name the non-maintained school they must name another school.

3. Parents *do not express a preference* for the individual special school to be named in their child's statement.

The LEA must consider the parent preference for a special school education. In doing so the LEA must have regard to section 9 of the Education Act 1996. This sets the general principle that pupils must be educated in accordance with parental wishes so far as this is compatible with the provision of efficient instruction and training and the avoidance of unreasonable public expenditure.

The LEA must also have regard to the need to arrange suitable special educational provision imposed by section 324 of the Education Act 1996.

The LEA decides which school is named in the child's statement.

The parents disagree or are unhappy about what the LEA has proposed. (This can occur at any time)

At any stage of the process parents can use the local informal disagreement resolution arrangements, which include an independent element, to seek to resolve any disputes. This service is entered into voluntarily and does not affect the right to lodge a formal appeal to the SEN Tribunal. Where parents disagree with the provision proposed in their child's statement (including the school or type of school) they can appeal to the SEN Tribunal. The local parent partnership service can provide advice and act as a signpost to these services.

The same procedures normally apply when parents ask for the school named in their child's statement to be changed.

Introduction and context

1   In **1993** the general principle that children with special educational needs should – where this is what parents wanted – normally be educated at mainstream schools was enshrined into law[1]. However, pupils and their families had to satisfy a series of conditions – the mainstream's ability to ensure the child received the educational provision his or her learning difficulty called for while also ensuring the efficient education of others with whom she or he would be educated and the efficient use of resources – before they secured access to mainstream education. These conditions were open to abuse and children who would have benefited from inclusion were denied access to mainstream education.

2   Like most countries in the world the United Kingdom supports the Salamanca Statement The statement drawn up by a UNESCO[2] world conference, held in Salamanca (Spain in **1994**) called upon all Governments to "adopt as a matter of law or policy the principle of inclusive education, enrolling all children in regular schools, unless there are compelling reasons for doing otherwise".

3   In **1997** the new Government published 'Excellence For All Children – Meeting Special Educational Needs'. This set out a strategy to improve standards for pupils with special educational needs. A clear commitment to promoting greater inclusion was signalled, as was the need to develop the role of special schools. In doing this the significant educational, social and moral benefits of inclusion were highlighted. Following substantial consultation 'Meeting Special Educational Needs – A Programme of Action' was published in **1998**. This undertook to review the statutory framework for inclusion in conjunction with the Disability Rights Task Force. The Task Force's report 'From Exclusion To Inclusion' – published in **1999** – recommended "a strengthened right for parents of children with statements of special educational needs[3] to a place at a mainstream school".

4   The Special Educational Needs and Disability Act **2001** delivers a strengthened right to a mainstream education for children with special educational needs. The Act has amended the Education Act 1996 and transformed the statutory framework for inclusion into a positive endorsement of inclusion. The Act seeks to enable more pupils who have special educational needs to be included successfully within mainstream education. This clearly signals that where parents want a mainstream education for their child everything possible should be done to provide it. Equally where parents want a special school place their wishes should be listened to and taken into account.

Status of the guidance

5   This is statutory guidance. It provides practical advice on the operation of the new inclusion framework. All maintained schools (including maintained nursery schools) and local education authorities, in England, must have regard to this guidance[4]. In addition, City Academies, in England, are also required to have regard to the guidance via their funding agreements with the

---

[1] The Education Act 1993 (section 160) which was subsequently consolidated into the Education Act 1996 (section 316).

[2] United Nations Education, Scientific and Cultural Organisation.

[3] As provided for by section 324 of the Education Act 1996. The SEN Code of Practice provides detailed information and advice on statements of special educational need.

[4] This is required by section 316A(8) of the Education Act 1996.

Secretary of State. **This means the guidance must not be ignored.** City Technology Colleges and City Colleges for the Technology of the Arts, in England, are also strongly encouraged to have regard to the guidance. The guidance is designed to help schools and local education authorities make effective decisions. Whilst it offers examples it does not – and could not – cover every situation that schools and local education authorities may have to face. The new statutory framework for inclusion comes into force on 1 January 2002. The new wording of sections 316 and 316A of the Education Act 1996 are set out at **annex A**.

Key principles

6   In seeking to develop inclusive education systems schools, local authorities and others should keep the following key principles in mind at all times. Readers should also have regard to the overall guidance provided in the Special Educational Needs Code of Practice[5] and the Disability Rights Commission's Code of Practice[6] on the new school disability duties (also see paragraph 10 below).

Principles of an inclusive education service

- Inclusion is a process by which schools, local education authorities and others develop their cultures, policies and practices to include pupils.
- With the right training, strategies and support nearly all children with special educational needs can be successfully included in mainstream education.
- An inclusive education service offers excellence and choice and incorporates the views of parents and children.
- The interests of all pupils must be safeguarded.
- Schools, local education authorities and others should actively seek to remove barriers to learning and participation.
- All children should have access to an appropriate education that affords them the opportunity to achieve their personal potential.
- Mainstream education will not always be right for every child all of the time. Equally just because mainstream education may not be right at a particular stage it does not prevent the child from being included successfully at a later stage.

Developing effective inclusion

7   Schools supported by local education authorities and others should actively seek to remove the barriers to learning and participation that can hinder or exclude pupils with special educational needs. Schools and local education authorities that are successful at including pupils with special educational needs meet those needs in a positive and proactive way. They also approach inclusion as part of their overall improvement strategy. Inclusion is far more than just about the location of a child's school placement.

---

[5] References to the SEN Code of Practice refer to the revised Code anticipated to come into force on 1 January 2002.

[6] The Disability Rights Commission issued (July 2001) a Draft Code of Practice (Schools).